BEHOLD
THE POWER OF
IGNORANCE

Tom,

Please continue to rock.

goats

BEHOLD
THE POWER OF
IGNORANCE

VOLUME IV

BY JONATHAN ROSENBERG

POINT E PUBLISHING

NEW YORK

FOR AMY
WHO HAS MANAGED TO PUT UP WITH ME QUITE WELL SO FAR

FOR MOM
YOU SQUOZE ME OUT REEL GUD

AND FOR DELFA ROLL DANISH RIBBONS
WITHOUT WHICH THIS BOOK WOULD NOT HAVE BEEN FREAKIN' POSSIBLE

❦ INTRODUCTION. ❦

Howdy, kids.

Right off the bat, I'd like to give a big welcome to those of you who are new to Goats, to those unfortunate souls who've had this volume thrust upon you by some sick, sadly insistent friend, family member or hospital patient. Goats is a comic strip chronicling the adventures of two hapless (i.e., without hap) antisocialites, their oversexed pet goat and their chaos-inclined pet chicken.

It is, of course, much more than that, but that's enough to get you started. If you continue on, you'll have the opportunity to meet some of their friends (animal, vegetable and alien alike) and the people, places and things inhabiting their slightly twisted universe. And if you choose to continue your journey with us once you've finished this collection, you are most cordially invited to join us for further gut-busting, bladder-clenching fun on the World Wide Internet at Goats.com. For those of you already familiar with our little family, wipe off your shoes, come on in, and grab a spot on the carpet by the fire.

Drawing a comic strip with as varied and diverse a cast of characters as Goats holds has (out of necessity) granted me the ability to enter a sort of self-induced state of schizophrenia. I become each of these characters as I write. Their dirty little thoughts contaminate my mind as we dance our unnatural tango. Their world is real to me. My job is simply to chronicle what I see there.

Occasionally, though, I wonder if I am not communicating every aspect of that world, if perhaps I have left something out due to eagerness or sluggishness or inattentiveness. I worry that you won't be able to see clearly that which is bubbling about in my mind, and I certainly worry that it will be misinterpreted. Leaving aside discussions of why I might harbor such neuroses, the simple fact is that Goats has reached an extraordinarily complex level of peculiarity over the (almost) five years that I've been drawing it, and without the proper context of all that's come before it, one might become truly, irrevocably confused by any given strip.

I wondered as I was putting this book together how a reader who hadn't first encountered the August 1998 series (available on the Goats.com website, or, if you're reading this in the far-flung future, probably lounging about on some sort of futuristic hovering pool float, applying your 3,000 SPF sunblock and keeping those huge, nasty flying mutant lizards out of your sun with the occasional blast of your phase pistol, in Volume II of this series of books) detailing the future escapades of robotic weasels, the Jello Wars, and a hovering, bodiless Bill Cosby's brain would interpret the "Elian: Tales of a First-Grade Assassin" strips contained somewhere within the following pages. It would be almost cruelly confusing, given that the stories aren't exactly straightforward even when read together.

It was at that moment that I knew I had made the right decision in releasing the fourth volume of the strip before the preceding ones. With the printing of this edition, one small victory has been won in the name of Universal Chaos.

Like George Lucas before me, I have released the fourth part of a longer tale first. Goats lacks the cohesive plot, intriguing characters and fascinating universe of Lucas' epic, but I have his love of money. By publishing this fourth collection first, we (and by 'we', I refer to myself and Goats' resourceful, slightly annoying programmer/business manager Phillip Karlsson) can cash in on the level of mediocrity we've managed to achieve thus far. Hopefully we can sell the following (or prior, depending on your perspective) books on previous reputation (and before the general public realizes just how awful they really are).

And, of course, I relish the idea that those aforementioned future-readers may look for the aforementioned Jello Wars series in the next book only to realize that Volume III was released second, and, in their consternation, that they might be eaten by a illiterate, unappreciative mutant lizard.

Of course, we don't actually wish our readers ill (at least, not until they stop purchasing merchandise). I get the occasional complaint from someone suffering from whiplash after having taken a run-on sentence too quickly or cornered into a digression without first coming to a full and complete stop, but none of these aches and pains are intentionally inflicted. The only thing we ask of our readers is that they enjoy them-selves, and, failing that, that complaints do not take the form of angry missives or thrown stones.

Your enjoyment (or, rather, my enjoyment and the enjoyment of like-minded individuals) is my only goal when I draw a strip. I'd like to think that I avoid falling into the typical traps that cartoonists can fall into en route to that goal. I'm not here to touch your heart or make you think about how short and precious life is. I'm not here to give you a comfortable place to return each weekday to smile blandly at the antics of one-dimensional characters in an unchanging world. I'm not here to make you think about anything serious for more than a fleeting moment, if possible. Lazy as I am, I'm sure that those cushy fallbacks are irresistible on occasion, but they're only temporary pit stops on the way to the next bizarre scenario. All I can hope is to provide a short respite from the everyday. And with that saccharine note, I hope you enjoy the following comic strips.

— Jonathan Rosenberg

EXCUSE ME, BUT I THINK THIS IS YOURS.

SO THAT'S WHERE YOU'VE BEEN OFF TO! NAUGHTY, NAUGHTY SEX DWARF.

UH UH UH!

I WOULD LIKE YOU ON A BLACK LEASH... I WOULD PARADE YOU DOWN THE HIGH STREETS! YOU'VE GOT THE ATTRACTION, YOU'VE GOT THE PULLING POWER... WALK MY LITTLE DOGGIE! WALK MY LITTLE SEX DWARF!!

THIS IS JUST SO WRONG.

YOU'RE TELLING ME. WHAT ABOUT MY NEEDS?

Jan. 25, 2000

jon@goats.com

BOB IS ABSOLUTELY OUT OF CONTROL WITH THIS SEX DWARF THING.

JEALOUS MUCH?

LIKE YOU WOULD BE ABLE TO SLEEP THROUGH ALL THAT INCESSANT POUNDING... SLIPPING ON EMPTY TUBES OF LUBRICANT SCATTERED ABOUT THE FLOOR, HAMSTER DROPPINGS CLOGGING THE SHIP'S FUEL INTAKE. THAT'S NOT LOVE... THAT'S... THAT'S...

TAINTED LOVE?

Jan. 26, 2000

jon@goats.com

INCON-SIDERATE.

AT LEAST HE DOESN'T LEAVE THE TOILET SEAT UP LIKE SOME PEOPLE.

QUIET.

IT SEEMS THAT THE GIANT ROBOT THAT HAS BEEN TERRORIZING NEW YORK HAS STOPPED ITS RAMPAGE, AS A STRANGE FAT BOY IN A CAPE HAS APPROACHED THE BEAST, HOLDING ONLY A CHESSBOARD. HE SEEMS TO BE SETTING UP THE BOARD, AS IF TO PLAY AGAINST THE ROBOT. WILL A SIMPLE GAME OF CHESS HELP END THE HORROR? LET'S GO THERE NOW.

CRUNCH.

OOH.

THAT'S GOTTA HURT.

WHO DIDN'T SEE THAT COMING?

IS CRUSHING YOUR OPPONENT A LEGAL MOVE?

WELL, ALL OUR EFFORTS TO STOP SEX DWARF HAVE FAILED, AND CHESSMASTER 2000 IS IN TRACTION FOR THE NEXT SIX MONTHS. I'M ALL OUT OF IDEAS.

WE COULD GIVE UP.

YOU MEAN, JUST LET SEX DWARF WIN? KEEP OUR ENGINE PARTS? DESTROY THE CITY?

UMM... YEAH.

MAN, I LOVE IT WHEN A PLAN COMES TOGETHER.

DEALING WITH PROBLEMS IS ONLY FOR PEOPLE TOO WEAK TO RUN AWAY FROM THEM.

FEB. 18, 2000

jonegoats.com

FEB. 21, 2000

jonegoats.com

February 28, 2000 Phillip

phillip@goats.com

February 29, 2000 Phillip

phillip@goats.com

AS YOU BOTH KNOW, I WAS ONCE HEAVILY INVOLVED IN THE EUROPEAN BOCCE CIRCUIT DUE TO THE INFLUENCE OF MY ONE-EYED, ROBOTIC-LIMBED FRENCHMAN FRIEND, SHAZAM TWIX. AFTER LOSING HIS JOB IN THE VINEYARDS OF EPERNAY DUE TO WHAT THE AUTHORITIES TERMED "EXCESSIVE DRUG USE," SPORT WAS HIS ONLY SOLACE.

HE DID RATHER WELL FOR HIMSELF ON THE CIRCUIT, AS MANY OF THE OTHER PLAYERS WERE OF SIMILAR CHARACTER, AND HELPED TO MASK HIS ECCENTRICITIES. DESPITE HIS TENDENCY TO BECOME SIDETRACKED IN DEBATES WITH INVISIBLE GIRAFFES, HE WAS AN EXEMPLARY PLAYER, AND RARELY LICKED ANYONE WITHOUT PRIOR PERMISSION.

MAR. 13, 2000

jon@goats.com

TWIX WAS RANKED THIRD ON THE CONTINENT UNTIL ONE FATEFUL EVENING, WHEN AFTER A PARTICULARLY FRENETIC BINGE HOPPED UP ON MAINLINED COCOA AND FETUS EXTRACT, HE ACCIDENTALLY ATE A REFEREE. SUCH THINGS WERE FROWNED UPON IN THE WORLD OF BOCCE.

AFTER A BRIEF BUT VIOLENT DISCUSSION WITH THE BOCCE TRIBUNAL, TWIX WAS BANISHED FROM THE SPORT FOR REFEREE CONSUMPTION AND EXCESSIVE FLATULENCE. HAVING FIRST LOST HIS JOB (AND ACCESS TO THE LUSCIOUS AND MORALLY-CHALLENGED CHAMPAGNE CELLAR TOUR GUIDES), AND NOW WITH HIS PRECIOUS BOCCE TAKEN AWAY, HE WAS CRUSHED.

MAR. 14, 2000

THE NEXT THREE MONTHS WERE AN ENDLESS TORMENT FOR BOTH TWIX AND MYSELF, AS I HAD TO REPEATEDLY TALK HIM DOWN FROM HIS EXPERIMENTATIONS WITH THE HALLUCINOGENIC EFFECTS OF HAM 'N' CHEESE HOT POCKET OVERDOSING. HE BABBLED ENDLESSLY ABOUT HIS "NEXT BIG THING."

jon@goats.com

AFTER TOYING WITH FLAWED (THE MONKEY FUND: A MUTUAL FUND RUN BY MONKEYS, INVESTING ONLY IN MONKEY-FRIENDLY STOCKS) AND HOPELESS (THE HOOTIE CHANNEL: ALL HOOTIE, ALL THE TIME) BUSINESS IDEAS, SHAZAM TWIX DECIDED TO RE-ENTER THE WORLD OF SPORT. BUT THIS TIME, HE WOULD RISE THROUGH THE RANKS OF HEAD-TO-HEAD ROLLER-BIATHLON.

IT WAS DECIDED THAT DAY THAT WE WOULD MOVE TO BRUSSELS, THE "NEW JERSEY OF EUROPE" AND THE UN-OFFICIAL HOME OF HEAD-TO-HEAD ROLLER-BIATHLON CULTURE. WE PACKED TWIX'S 1981 MERCURY ZEPHYR WITH THE MEAGER CONTENTS OF OUR SQUATTER'S FLAT (A TOILET BRUSH, A VARIETY OF SPORTING GOODS, AND 15 KILOS OF NUTELLA) AND HEADED FOR BELGIUM.

LIFE ON THE ROAD WAS GRAND... THERE WERE SHEEP... AND SOME ADDITIONAL SHEEP... MAN, THERE WERE A LOT OF SHEEP. THEY WERE EVERYWHERE. PRETTY MUCH A SHEEP ANYWHERE YOU LOOKED. THEY ATE GRASS AND WALKED AROUND A BIT.

MAR. 15, 2000

I GUESS IT'S HARD TO KEEP THE ACTION FLOWING WHEN YOU'RE MAKING STUFF UP ON THE SPOT.

I AM NOT. SHEEP ARE INTEGRAL TO THE TONE OF THE STORY.

WERE THE SHEEP BEAUTIFUL?

jon@goats.com

AFTER SEVERAL DAYS OF ADVENTURE ON THE ROAD (AND A QUICK STOP AT "MINI-EUROPE" FOR PHOTOS), WE ARRIVED AT OUR NEW FLAT IN BRUSSELS, OVERLOOKING THE GRAND-PLACE. GETTING INTO THE SPIRIT OF THE CITY, TWIX SHARED HIS "MANNEKEN PIS" IMPRESSION WITH THE TOURISTS BELOW OUR BALCONY.

AFTER UNLOADING THE ZEPHYR, WE STRUCK OUT ON THE COBBLESTONE STREETS OF THE CITY, LOOKING FOR FRITES AND HEAD-TO-HEAD ROLLER-BIATHLON SPARRING PARTNERS. WE FOUND FRITES; IT WAS SOMEWHAT HARDER TO FIND PEOPLE WILLING TO TAKE A BULLET IN THE NAME OF SPORT.

MAR. 16, 2000

AS WE WALKED, THE BRIGHT PINK OF A PHOTOCOPIED FLYER TAPED TO A LAMPPOST CAUGHT MY EYE. I PLUCKED IT FROM THE POST. IT WAS AN ADVERTISEMENT FOR THE UPCOMING ROLLER-BIATHLON TOURNAMENT, TO BE HELD RIGHT THERE IN BRUSSELS, TWO WEEKS FROM THE DAY. I TURNED TO SHOW TWIX, BUT HE WAS NOWHERE TO BE SEEN.

jon@goats.com

SUDDENLY, I FOUND MYSELF AS ALONE AS A FAT GIRL ON A FRIDAY NIGHT.* SHAZAM TWIX WAS GONE, WITH ONLY A FEW ODDLY-SHAPED LEAVES BLOWING IN CIRCLES ON THE GROUND WHERE HE HAD STOOD MOMENTS BEFORE. IT WAS GETTING DARK, AND I FELT A PRESSING NEED TO GET OFF THE STREETS.

*NO, I'M NOT CALLING YOU FAT. GET OVER YOURSELF.

I DUCKED INTO A NEARBY BAR, APTLY NAMED "PLANET COCKTAIL BAR". IT WAS PACKED WITH GREASY BELGIANS SIPPING FRUIT-LADEN DRINKS, SWAYING TO TRANCE-INDUCING HOUSE MUSIC. YOU WILL NEVER FIND A MORE WRETCHED HIVE OF SCUM AND VILLAINY THAN PLANET COCKTAIL BAR.

MAR. 17, 2000

jonegoats.com

I ORDERED MY CUSTOMARY LONG ISLAND ICED TEA, AND SAT MYSELF DOWN IN A BOOTH WITH THREE BLONDE BELGIAN BEAUTIES. I SPOKE TO THEM THE ONLY FRENCH PHRASE THAT TWIX HAD TAUGHT ME: "I, TOO, ENJOY THE SOCCER."

BUT THOSE FIVE WORDS WERE MORE THAN ENOUGH...

HAVING READ AS MUCH BRUSSELS-SPECIFIC TOURIST LITERATURE AS POSSIBLE, I WAS KEENLY AWARE OF THE NATIVE REVERENCE FOR THE ART OF COMICS. I WAS ALSO KEENLY AWARE THAT BELGIANS WERE AS EASY AS MAC 'N' CHEESE. I PLIED THE BUXOM BLONDES WITH TALES OF MY CAREER AS A COMIC STRIPPER BACK IN THE STATES.

MAR. 20, 2000

MY THREE DATES WERE SO OVERWHELMED BY MY STUNNING (ALBEIT FABRICATED) REVELATION THAT THEY IMMEDIATELY INVITED ME BACK TO THEIR SORORITY HOUSE FOR A SWEATY, STICKY THREE-WAY. JUST THEN, I NO-TICED YET ANOTHER OF THOSE ODDLY-SHAPED LEAVES ON THE FLOOR OF THE BAR.

jonegoats.com

MY MIND RETURNED TO SHAZAM TWIX AND HIS DISAPPEARANCE. I RECALLED THE WORDS HE HAD SPOKEN TO ME JUST THAT MORNING: "TOAST IS JUST OVER-COOKED BREAD." AND I KNEW THEN THAT HE WAS RIGHT. DETERMINED TO FIND TWIX, I SENT THE GIRLS ON THEIR WAY WITH ONLY MY PROMISE TO CALL THEM.

SOMETHING ABOUT THE ODDLY-SHAPED LEAVES TRIGGERED A MEMORY. ON A HUNCH, I FOLLOWED THE TRAIL OF LEAVES TOWARDS THE BACK OF PLANET COCKTAIL BAR, THROUGH A BRIGHTLY-COLORED BEADED CURTAIN. THE BEADS WERE PRETTY. PRETTY, PRETTY BEADS.

WERE THEY PRETTY IN THE WAY THAT POST-NOSE JOB JENNIFER GREY IS PRETTY?

MORE IN A FULLY-LOADED PIZZA SORT OF WAY.

HELLO? STORY?

MAR. 21, 2000

I THINK SHE WAS PRETTIER BEFORE THE NOSE JOB.

JON, I THINK YOU COULD STAND TO RELAX A BIT.

DIABLO, I THINK YOU'VE BEEN SMOKING TOO MANY OF THOSE ODDLY-SHAPED LEAVES.

jon@goats.com

I PULLED ASIDE THE BEADED CURTAIN. THERE, IN THE BACK ROOM OF PLANET COCKTAIL BAR, WAS NONE OTHER THAN MY NEMESIS, THE EVIL GREGOR MENDEL, FATHER OF MODERN GENETICS AND EX-WRESTLING CHAMPION!

MAR. 22, 2000

HOW DID HE SURVIVE THE EXPLOSION WITH WHICH WE HAD DESTROYED HIS LABORATORY? WHAT WAS HE DOING HERE IN BRUSSELS? WHY DID HIS SKIN NOW HAVE AN EERIE GREEN TINGE TO IT? HAD I REMEMBERED TO TURN OFF THE OVEN THAT MORNING? AND WHAT HAD HE DONE WITH SHAZAM TWIX?

jon@goats.com

"AH, DIABLO, MY FRIEND," THE EVIL ONE INTONED, HIS HANDS RUBBING TOGETHER LIKE TWO HORNY, INCESTUOUS TECTONIC PLATES. "FINALLY, A CHANCE FOR US TO HAVE THAT DIM-SUM WE TALKED ABOUT SO LONG AGO. COME, AND HAVE SOME OF MY STICKY BALLS."

MENDEL SETTLED BACK INTO HIS SEAT AND BEGAN TO TALK. "OUR LAST, SHALL WE SAY, 'EXPLOSIVE' ENCOUNTER LEFT ME WITH SEVERE BURNS OVER 90% OF MY BODY. I STITCHED MYSELF TOGETHER OVER FIVE MONTHS OF PAINFUL GENETICALLY-ENGINEERED PLANT-SKIN TRANSPLANTS."

"FIVE MONTHS OF TORTUROUS PAIN IS A LONG TIME, DIABLO. FIVE MONTHS OF NOTHING BUT PONDERING REVENGE AGAINST YOU AND YOUR FRIEND TWIX. THAT, AND READING 'NEWSWEEK.' AND SAMPLING DIFFERENT VARIETIES OF BEN 'N' JERRY'S WONDERFUL ICE CREAM FLAVORS."

MAR. 23, 2000

"AND, OF COURSE, THE OCCASIONAL GAME OF YAHTZEE, BUT, AS WE ALL KNOW, MY SENTIENT PEA-PLANT HENCHMEN AREN'T VERY GOOD GAME PLAYERS, SO THERE WAS LITTLE CHALLENGE THERE. THEY OFTEN ATE THE DICE. BUT MOSTLY, I PONDERED REVENGE. REVENGE AND MONKEYS. MONKEYS ARE FUNNY."

jon@goats.com

MENDEL CHEWED THOUGHTFULLY ON HIS PORK BUNS. "ONCE I HAD RECOVERED FROM THE SKIN TRANS-PLANTS, I FOUND THAT I NO LONGER HAD THE UPPER-BODY STRENGTH TO MAINTAIN MY WRESTLING CAREER. ONLY THE SOLACE OF THRICE-DAILY PINTS OF 'PHISH FOOD' KEPT ME FROM SLIPPING INTO PERMANENT DEPRESSION."

MAR. 24, 2000

"I NEEDED A NEW WAY TO GENERATE INCOME TO FUND MY GENETIC ENGINEERING, WORLD-DOMINATION AND REVENGE-RELATED ACTIVITIES. I DID A BRIEF STINT AT THE HOME 'N' GARDEN DEPARTMENT OF 'HOME DESPOT,' BUT $6.20 AN HOUR DOESN'T GO AS FAR NOW AS IT DID BACK IN THE 1800s."

jon@goats.com

"CLEARLY, I NEEDED A NEW SPORT TO DOMINATE — A SPORT THAT CATERED TO MY VIOLENT IMPULSES AND LOVE FOR PHALLIC SYMBOLISM. A SPORT DRIPPING IN CASH AND BLOOD. I DECIDED THEN THAT I WOULD CONQUER THE WORLD OF HEAD-TO-HEAD ROLLER-BIATHLON."

MENDEL CONTINUED HIS SPIEL. "OF COURSE, NOW THAT YOU AND TWIX HAVE CONVENIENTLY DELIVERED YOURSELVES TO ME, MY ELABORATE PLANS FOR REVENGE HAVE BEEN FOILED. BUT, AS I AM A SOMEWHAT SPORTING VILLAIN, AND NOT ALTOGETHER BRIGHT, I SUGGEST WE HAVE A SMALL COMPETITION."

MAR. 27, 2000

"WE WILL PIT MY ARMY OF ROBOTIC BASKETBALL PLAYERS AGAINST YOUR BELOVED HARLEM GLOBETROTTERS. THE LOSER WILL BE KILLED, AND THE WINNER WILL BE GIVEN THE DEED TO GILLIGAN'S ISLAND." I REMINDED MENDEL THAT HE HAD NEITHER THE ROBOTS NOR THE DEED TO THE FICTIONAL ISLE.

jon@goats.com

AFTER SOME DISCUSSION, WE AGREED THAT MENDEL AND TWIX WOULD MEET IN DEADLY COMBAT AT THE UPCOMING HEAD-TO-HEAD ROLLER-BIATHLON COMPETITION, DECIDING ONCE AND FOR ALL WHO WOULD REIGN OVER THE H.T.H.R.B.L, AND WHO WOULD PERISH.

MENDEL'S HENCHMEN RETURNED SHAZAM TWIX TO ME, SOMEWHAT BATTERED BUT WITHOUT ANY PERMANENT DAMAGE. WE RETIRED TO OUR BRUSSELS FLAT, WHERE TWIX BEGAN THE RECOVERY PROCESS WITH A BONGFUL OF CHEX MIX AND TABASCO SAUCE.

MAR. 28, 2000

THE TWO-WEEK TRAINING PERIOD BEGAN IN EARNEST THE FOLLOWING DAY. I PUT TWIX ON A STRICT DIET OF CHINESE TAKE-OUT (BEEF PORK WITH CHICKEN) AND "LEMUR PATROL" CEREAL (MARSHMALLOWS SHAPED LIKE MILITANT LEMURS, PART OF THIS COMPLETE BREAKFAST.)

jon@goats.com

TWIX'S TRAINING REGIMEN CONSISTED OF DAILY STROLLS THROUGH THE NEIGHBORHOOD PARK (ARMED WITH A QUIVER OF BAGUETTES IN CASE OF MIME ATTACK) AND FREQUENT GAMES OF SKI-BALL AT "EDDIE'S WORLD OF SKI-BALL." TWIX WON A STUFFED SALAMANDER.

THE TOURNAMENT WAS BRUTAL. CONCESSIONS SALES WERE SLOW.

MAR. 29, 2000

THE TWO SURVIVING COMBATANTS, TWIX AND MENDEL, STEPPED INTO THE ARENA TO FACE OFF FOR THE HEAD-TO-HEAD ROLLER-BIATHLON FINALS. THE TENSION WAS AS THICK AS A COMMUNITY COLLEGE STUDENT. THE REFEREE BLEW HIS WHISTLE, AND THE MATCH BEGAN.

MAR. 30, 2000

"BLAM"
"BLAM"

jon@goats.com

OVERTIME IS RARELY A CONCERN IN HEAD-TO-HEAD ROLLER-BIATHLON.

WELL, WE WERE WORRIED FOR A WHILE, BUT ELIAN IS BACK, AND NONE THE WORSE FOR WEAR.

SEIS SEIS SEIS MORIR MORIR

LIVE

MAY 4, 2000

ELIAN, ARE YOU CONCERNED THAT THE DELAY IN YOUR RETURN TO CUBA WILL WORSEN INTERNATIONAL RELATIONS AND PUSH US CLOSER TO A STATE OF WAR?

MORIR FORNICAR MORIR

LIVE

HE MAY BE CONFUSED, BUT ONE THING IS FOR SURE: ELIAN IS NOT A ROBOTIC AUTOMATON FROM THE FUTURE BENT ON WORLD DOMINATION.

MORIR MORIR MORIR

jon@goats.com

...AND SO, OUR TALE OF ASSASSINS, WEASELS, ROBOTS, AND CHILD CUSTODY COMES TO A CLOSE. FOR NOW.

WE NOW RETURN YOU TO YOUR REGULARLY SCHEDULED STORYLINE, ALREADY IN PROGRESS.

MAY 5, 2000

JON. WE'RE ON.

OH. AH... WELL, THAT SURE WAS A WACKY ADVENTURE I HAD WITH... UM... VANESSA. YEAH.

YES. IT WAS VERY WACKY. AND ZANY.

jon@goats.com

GREAT. DIABLO AND JERRELL COMPLETELY TRASHED OUR NAVIGATIONAL COMPUTERS.

NOW WE'LL HAVE TO WANDER SPACE AIMLESSLY, LOOKING FOR A WAY HOME.

OOH! I CAN BE MATT LE BLANC, AND YOU CAN BE HEATHER GRAHAM.

MAY 24, 2000

WHY CAN'T YOU BE HEATHER GRAHAM?

'CAUSE I'M NOT THE ONE THAT LOST THAT GAME OF "SOGGY BISCUIT" THIS AFTERNOON.

jon@goats.com

AND SO, OUR HEROES SET OFF ON A QUEST TO FIND THEIR WAY HOME... A QUEST THAT WOULD BRING THEM IN CONTACT WITH A CIVILIZATION OF CONDENSED MONKEYS...

MAY 25, 2000

...A QUEST WHERE THEY WOULD DISCOVER THE FABLED "HAMSTER OF KNOWLEDGE" OF KRONOS VII ...

I DON'T FEEL ANY SMARTER, BUT IT'S JERY COMFORTABLE.

jon@goats.com

...AND A QUEST THAT WOULD BRING THEM INTO THE INEVITABLE BLOODY CONFLICT WITH GARY OLDMAN.

I'M QUITE EVIL.

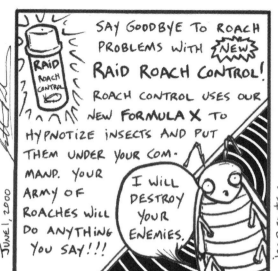

I KEEP HEARING VOICES IN MY HEAD, TELLING ME TO KILL THE OTHERS... THE HERETICS. IT'S BEGINNING TO AFFECT MY JOB PERFORMANCE, MY SOCIAL LIFE, AND I DON'T SLEEP VERY WELL AT NIGHT. WHAT'S A WELL-MEANING PSYCHOPATH TO DO?

JUNE 5, 2000

KEEP THOSE PESKY VOICES OUT OF YOUR HEAD WITH NEW EXTRA-STRENGTH **TREPAN-A!** TREPAN-A GETS RID OF THE EVIL SPIRITS IN YOUR BRAIN, ALLOWING YOU TO REJOIN OUR CONSUMER SOCIETY.

YOUR BRAIN

PESKY SKULL

EVIL SPIRITS

TREPAN-A

jon@goats.com

THINKING NO HARD NOW. THANKS, TREPAN-A!

ASK YOUR DOCTOR ABOUT TREPAN-A TODAY.

TREPAN-A©

OPEN YOUR MIND.

SOMETIMES I HAVE AN ACCIDENT. AND THAT'S OKAY, 'CAUSE MOMMY SAYS I'M A GOOD BOY. BUT AT THE END OF A LONG DAY, I'D LOVE TO BE ABLE TO REMOVE THE EXCESS FECES FROM MY BUTTOCKS. UNTIL NOW, IT WASN'T POSSIBLE.

JUNE 6, 2000

THAT'S WHERE **SHARMIN** COMES IN. SHARMIN TOILET TISSUE REMOVES EXCESS FECES WITHOUT THE USE OF ABRASIVES OR HARSH CHEMICALS, SO MY FLESHY CHEEKS REMAIN SMOOTH AND UNBLOODIED. AND IT'S MADE FROM ALL-NATURAL BABY SKIN, SO YOU KNOW IT'S GOOD FOR THE ENVIRONMENT.

jon@goats.com

Sharmin

MADE BABY-SOFT 'CAUSE IT'S MADE FROM BABIES.

IT FEELS GOOD.

YOU GOT YOUR FOOD FROM A TRUCK?

HOT TRUCK ISN'T JUST A TRUCK, LAUREN... IT'S AN INSTITUTION. BOB'S BEEN SERVING UP TASTY SUBS FOR 40 YEARS NOW.

JUN. 30, 2000

I CAN'T MAKE HEADS OR TAILS OF THE MENU.

IT'S EASY. FOR EXAMPLE, I'M ORDERING A DOUBLE P.M.P. EXTRA WET EXTRA HEAVY SOPRANO GREASE & GARDEN LIQUID HEAT ONION BBQ.

I ASSUME ALL THOSE WORDS HAVE ENGLISH TRANSLATIONS.

MAYBE. I THINK THIS IS THE FIRST TIME I'VE BEEN HERE SOBER.

jon@goats.com

THE FALL CREEK GORGE... A MIRACLE OF NATURE RUNNING RIGHT THROUGH CAMPUS. IT TOOK THOUSANDS OF YEARS FOR A TRICKLE OF WATER TO CARVE THIS.

ABOUT THE SAME TIME IT'S TAKING ME TO FIND ANY ACTION.

JUL. 3, 2000

AN OASIS OF ROCK, FLORA, AND FLOWING WATER. IT'S LIKE... IT'S LIKE I'M TALKING TO MYSELF.

jon@goats.com

EXPLAIN THIS "SKINNY DIPPING" THING I KEEP HEARING ABOUT.

IT'D BE EASIER TO DEMONSTRATE.

GET CRAIG IN HERE IMMEDIATELY... I'M GOING TO NEED HIM TO MAKE AN ANNOUNCEMENT TO THE PRESS.

AUG. 1, 2000

AND PUT THE ATTORNEYS ON ALERT. I'LL BE NEEDING THEM AS WELL.

ANYTHING ELSE, MASTER?

jon@goats.com

YES. FIND OUT WHY IT'S SO DAMNED DARK IN HERE.

YOU TURNED THE LIGHTS OFF, MASTER.

WELCOME TO NBC NIGHTLY NEWS. I'M TOM BROKAW. TODAY, DR. J. CRAIG VENTER, HEAD OF CELERA GENOMICS, ANNOUNCED THAT HIS COMPANY HAS PATENTED THE HUMAN GENOME.

AUG. 2, 2000

"I THINK IT'S UNDERSTANDABLE THAT WE WOULD WANT TO PATENT OUR ASSEMBLY OF THE GENOME," VENTER SAID AT TODAY'S PRESS CONFERENCE. "OF COURSE, ANYONE USING THE HUMAN GENOME WITHOUT AUTHORIZATION WILL HAVE TO STOP IMMEDIATELY."

jon@goats.com

DISPUTING CLAIMS THAT GOD HAS A CLAIM TO PRIOR ART, U.S. PATENT OFFICIALS SAID THAT GOD HAS 30 DAYS TO FILE A COUNTER-CLAIM. GOD COULD NOT BE REACHED FOR COMMENT.

HAVE YOU READ THE PAPER TODAY?

YEAH. THAT BIT ABOUT CHARLTON HESTON IN REHAB HAD ME ROLLING.

NO, THE ARTICLE ABOUT CELERA. THEY'VE PATENTED THE HUMAN GENOME.

SO? IT'S NOT MY GENOME.

AUG. 3, 2000

DIABLO, I'M GOING TO HAVE TO RETURN MY GENES TO CELERA.

IF YOU'VE ALREADY WORN THEM, THEY'LL PROBABLY ONLY GIVE YOU STORE CREDIT.

jon@goats.com

JON, I'VE BEEN DOING SOME RESEARCH ON THIS WHOLE GENOME PATENT THING, AND IT REEKS OF MY OLD NEMESIS, GREGOR MENDEL. ONLY HE WOULD DENY PEOPLE THE USE OF THEIR OWN GENETIC MATERIAL.

AUG. 4, 2000

MENDEL'S BEEN DEAD FOR 116 YEARS, DIABLO. I LOOKED IT UP.

BUT WHEN YOU REARRANGE THE LETTERS IN J. CRAIG VENTER'S NAME, IT SPELLS "GREGOR MENDEL." SEE?

jon@goats.com

NO IT DOESN'T. IT SPELLS OUT "RAVING REJECT," THOUGH.

YEAH, BUT THAT'S NOT MUCH OF A NAME FOR A NEMESIS.

August 10, 3:21pm
Toothgnip and I have disguised ourselves as Celera stormtroopers and stowed away on board one of their transports. If our efforts fail, this journal will be the only record of our heroic efforts.

August 10, 3:44pm
In a valiant effort to stave off boredom, Toothgnip and I have taken to playing "Rock, paper, scissors." A lack of fingers on both our parts has made the game rather difficult to play.

August 10, 3:57pm
Toothgnip has declined my offer to play poker. His excuse: "We have no cards." I think the stress of our upcoming siege may play a part in his reticence as well. I will attempt to engage him in a game of checkers.

WHAT ARE YOU DOING?

OH... JUST GOING OUT FOR A BIT.

Aug. 15, 2000

AND WHERE EXACTLY WERE YOU PLANNING ON GOING?

WE'RE GONNA ROCK DOWN TO ELECTRIC AVENUE.

jon@goats.com

AND THEN, I SUPPOSE, YOU'LL TAKE IT HIGHER.

MOST LIKELY.

WE CAUGHT THESE FOUR TRYING TO ESCAPE THE PRISONER CAMP.

EXCELLENT WORK. BRING THE MALES DOWN TO THE LABS AND PREP THEM.

Aug. 16, 2000

AND THE FEMALES?

UP TO MENDEL'S PRIVATE QUARTERS... JABBA TREATMENT.

jon@goats.com

JIMMY'S NOT UP TO PLAYING "RANCOR BEAST," SIR. HE HAS THE SNIFFLES.

THE GOLD BIKINIS WILL BE SUFFICIENT, SOLDIER.

LOOKS LIKE EVERYTHING'S BACK TO NORMAL... THE PRISONERS WERE RELEASED, CELERA'S GENOME PATENT HAS BEEN REVOKED, AND J. CRAIG VENTER WAS SENTENCED TO 30 YEARS IN A ROLL OF BOUNTY PAPER TOWELS.

BUT WHAT ABOUT MENDEL?

NO EVIDENCE WAS FOUND LINKING THE INCIDENT TO LONG-DEAD GENETICISTS, DIABLO.

I SUPPOSE YOU THINK THE GOLD BIKINIS WERE IMAGINARY, TOO.

NOPE. THOSE ARE INDELIBLY ETCHED INTO MY BRAIN.

AUG. 25, 2000

WHATCHA DOIN'?

I'M DRAWING A PARODY OF A FAMOUS TRADEMARK IN A DELIBERATE ATTEMPT TO DRAW THE WRATH OF CORPORATE LAWYERS.

WHAT'S THE DRAWING OF?

FECES™ BRAND PENIS BUTTER CUPS.

I'VE NEVER SEEN CANDY WITH SO MANY NIPPLES ON IT.

YOU CAN NEVER HAVE TOO MANY NIPPLES.

AUG. 28, 2000

Now that I've scanned my trademark parody, I can post it on my website. Lawyers should be swarming within minutes.

My keen wit and inflammatory statements are being seen by millions around the globe.

Lawyers were quicker back in my day.

Maybe you didn't draw enough nipples.

I'm not paying for lawyers this time, Diablo.

Corporations are the new government, Jon. We have to stand up to them.

Parody is the strongest form of social commentary, and corporations are trying to quash it with their fat wallets. Important political statements are going unheard by the public.

And what statement are you making by drawing nipples on a candy bar?

I wouldn't expect you to understand the subtleties.

Aug. 29, 2000

jon@goats.com

Aug. 30, 2000

jon@goats.com

HOW GOES THE LAWYER- BAITING?

NO BITES JUST YET.

IT'S TIME TO ESCALATE THE SITUATION.

CORPORATE LAWYERS ♥LOVE♥ Feces™ BRAND PENIS BUTTER CUPS

WE'RE TALKIN' TO YOU, WEASELNUTS.

AUG. 31, 2000

DO YOU KNOW ANYTHING ABOUT THAT BILLBOARD OUTSIDE?

I KNOW I HAVEN'T HEARD FROM A SINGLE LAW- YER ABOUT IT. VERY DISAP- POINTING.

SEPT. 1, 2000

THAT'S A GOOD THING, DIABLO.

THEY'RE TRAMPLING ON MY RIGHT TO CREATE SCANDAL AND BENEFIT FROM THE FREE PUBLICITY.

I DON'T THINK THAT'S A GUARANTEED RIGHT.

WHO THE HELL ARE YOU? CALISTA FLOCKHART?

jon@goats.com

HUMPA LUMPA PUMPADEE DOO,
I'VE GOT SOME LEGAL ADVICE FOR YOU.
HUMPA LUMPA PUMPADAH DEE,
HIRE AN ATTORNEY, A LAWYER OR THREE!

WHAT DO YOU GET WITH YOUR ARROGANT ART?
CEASE AND DESIST IS JUST FOR A START.
THE RIGHT TO FREE SPEECH ISN'T ENTIRELY FREE.
IT GOES TO THE ONES WITH TONS OF MONEY!

WHY WOULD YOU WANT TO
MAKE FUN OF CANDY?
SPEECH IS MOST DANGEROUS
WHEN IT IS FREE!

SAY WHAT YOU WILL ABOUT BUSH OR AL GORE,
MESS WITH BIG MONEY AND
WE'LL SHOW YOU THE DOOR!

HUMPA LUMPA PUMPADEE DAH
IF YOU SPEAK UP THEN WE'LL
OWN YOUR CAR,
YOU WILL LIVE IN POVERTY TOO,
LIKE THE HUMPA LUMPA
PUMPADEE DO!

SEPT. 5, 2000

DIABLO BROUGHT SOME CHOCOLATE FROM WORK. WANT SOME?

NO THANKS... CHOCOLATE MAKES ME BREAK OUT.

SEPT. 12, 2000

OH, C'MON. A FEW PIMPLES COULDN'T BE ANY WORSE THAN THE BOILS ON YOUR ASS.

THOSE ARE BEAUTY-MARKS.

jon@goats.com

BEAUTY MARKS DON'T OOZE PUS.

HOW DO YOU KNOW SO MUCH ABOUT MY ASS?

...ALL I'M SAYING IS THAT IF A CHICKEN CAN GET AN EXECUTIVE POSITION AT A COMPANY, WE SHOULD BE ABLE TO DO BETTER THAN THIS.

SEPT. 13, 2000

WHAT PAYS WELL AND DOESN'T REQUIRE ANY SKILL OR TALENT?

WE COULD BE FINANCIAL ANALYSTS.

jon@goats.com

I DON'T KNOW A THING ABOUT INVESTING.

THE ONLY THING YOU HAVE TO INVEST IN IS A MONKEY AND A DARTBOARD.

WELL, AS LONG AS WE'RE LOOKING FOR NEW JOBS, WE MIGHT AS WELL DO SOMETHING GLAMOROUS AND EXCITING.

GLAMOROUS LIKE A MOVIE STAR, OR EXCITING LIKE AN INTERNATIONAL SPY?

LIKE A CARTOONIST!

SEPT. 14, 2000

YOU'RE SUPPOSED TO OPEN THE WINDOWS WHILE YOU'RE CLEANING.

IT SMELLS LIKE STRAWBERRIES.

jon@goats.com

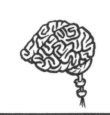

THIS IS YOUR BRAIN.

THIS IS YOUR BRAIN ON FRENCH TOAST.

THIS IS YOUR BRAIN ON A LLAMA.

SEPT. 15, 2000

THIS IS YOUR BRAIN ON A NUN.

jon@goats.com

STOP THAT.

WE HAD SOME LEFTOVER INVENTORY.

FISH'S ADVENTURE JOURNAL, DAY 1: FOR THE FIRST TIME IN TWO AND A HALF YEARS, I HAVE LEFT MY BEER MUG. FINALLY, I AM ON MY ADVENTURE.

SEPT. 22, 2000

FROM THIS HIGH PLACE, I CAN SEE FARTHER THAN I HAVE EVER SEEN BEFORE. I CAN FEEL THE WIND ON MY SCALES. I AM FREE!

jon@goats.com

YOU READY TO COME DOWN?

FIVE MORE MINUTES.

CHERISE IS HAVING A TOPLESS ROOFTOP PARTY. INTERESTED?

NAH. THINK I'M JUST GONNA PAY THE TAB AND HEAD HOME.

SEPT. 25, 2000

WHERE DO YOU GET THE CASH FOR THESE ALCOHOLIC EXTRAVAGANZAS, ANYWAY?

THROUGH THE MAGIC OF DEBIT CARDS, MY FRIEND.

jon@goats.com

THOSE ARE GENERALLY LINKED TO CHECKING ACCOUNTS.

I DON'T BOTHER THE BANK ABOUT SMALL DETAILS, AND THEY DON'T BOTHER ME.

WHAT WOMEN SAY:

I MEAN, HE'S GETTING AN APARTMENT, AND HE HASN'T EVEN TOLD ME? IT'S NOT AS IF I'M DEFINITELY READY TO MOVE IN WITH HIM, BUT DON'T YOU THINK IT'S SO[...]WE COULD HAV[...]SSED TOGETHE[...]

OCT. 4, 2000

WHAT GOATS HEAR:

I AM EMOTIONALLY VULNERABLE.

APOLOGIES TO GARY LARSON

SO PHILLIP'S BUYING AN APARTMENT, AND HE HASN'T ASKED YOU TO MOVE IN WITH HIM?

HE HASN'T EVEN TOLD ME.

OCT. 5, 2000

WELL, DO YOU WANT TO LIVE WITH HIM?

WELL, EVENTUALLY, BUT... NO. I GUESS NOT.

jon@goats.com

PERFECT. YOU'LL WANT TO FOLLOW PLAN R-15.

SLIGHT GUILT FOLLOWED BY A BIT OF SUBTLE MANIPULATION. I LIKE.

HERE. PUT THIS ON.

WHITE AFTER LABOR DAY? REALLY, PHILLIP, HOW TACKY.

IT'S A BLINDFOLD. I HAVE A SURPRISE FOR YOU.

YOU'RE NOT GOING TO PUT ON THOSE LEATHER CHAPS AND MAKE ME CALL YOU "FRITZ", ARE YOU?

OCT. 11, 2000

IT'S NOT LIKE THAT. WE'RE GOING OUTSIDE.

YOU'RE NOT VERY REASSURING, PHILLIP.

jon@goats.com

OKAY... JUST A FEW MORE STEPS...

AND TAKE OFF THE BLINDFOLD.

OCT. 12, 2000

OH PHILLIP... IT'S BEAUTIFUL.

IT'S THE TERRACE FOR MY NEW APART-MENT. NOW YOU WON'T HAVE TO LEAVE THE CITY TO ENJOY A BIT OF NATURE.

jon@goats.com

THANK YOU, PHILLIP. I LOVE IT.

GOOD, BECAUSE IF YOU LEAVE NEW YORK, THE DEATHS OF ALL THOSE HYDRANGEAS WILL BE ON YOUR HANDS.

LOOK, IF YOU'RE GOING TO ACCUSE ME OF BEING A LAPSED SATANIST, YOU'D BETTER SLAP ON A YARMULKE AND START CONSERVING PORK BEFORE THE HYPOCRISY PATROL COMES AND LOCKS YOU AWAY.

OCT. 19, 2000

THAT'S NOT WHAT I'M SAYING.

SO WHAT ARE YOU SAYING?

jon@goats.com

I... I DON'T EVEN KNOW ANYMORE.

AND YET, YOUR LIPS KEEP MOVING.

OKAY, MR. LESS-HOLIER-THAN-THOU, I'LL SHOW YOU THE TRUE POWER OF LUCIFER. I'M GOING TO RESURRECT YOUR WORST NIGHTMARE.

OCT. 20, 2000

jon@goats.com

OKAY, EVERYONE, YOU KNOW THE DRILL... WHEN THE ZOMBIE ENTERS, TAKE COVER AND PLACE YOUR HEAD BETWEEN YOUR LEGS. OR YOUR NEAREST NEIGHBOR'S LEGS.

BOOM

OCT. 27, 2000

SHE WON'T BE GETTING IN THROUGH THE BATHROOM.

EXCELLENT WORK.

jon@goats.com

SHE'S HERE! SHE'S HERE!

OKAY, EVERYBODY... GET TO YOUR STATIONS. AND GET READY TO KICK SOME ZOMBIE ASS.

OCT. 30, 2000

jon@goats.com

CARTOON CASTING CAN BE A SPIKY, RUST-LADEN PIT OF LEGAL COMPLICATIONS AND BRUISED EGOS. COME JOIN US AS WE GO SPELUNKING...

BEHIND the SCENES

DAY 2: GRETCHEN AND HEIDI

GOATS WAS THE BEST TIME OF MY LIFE... THE DRUGS, THE GROUPIES, THE FREE ACCORDION TUNINGS. JON SAID I'D NEVER NEED LOOK FOR ANOTHER JOB.

Nov. 6, 2000

jon@goats.com

THAT IS, UNTIL JUDY TENUTA'S LAWYERS CAME CALLING. I WAS DROPPED QUICKER THAN GEORGE W. IN A HONDA WITH A FIFTH OF JACK DANIELS. I'M WORKING PART-TIME AT "TINA'S HALLMARK."

THE PRESSURE OF INSTANT CELEBRITY OFTEN CLAIMS THE INNOCENCE OF AN UNWITTING YOUTH. LIKE OIL AND VINEGAR, DRUGS AND FAME JUST DON'T MIX...

BEHIND the SCENES

DAY 3: BIFF WELLINGTON

GODDAMN DISPOSABLE LIGHTERS... I FRIGGIN' GO THROUGH THREE OF THESE A WEEK. MAN, I'D KILL FOR SOME CHEETOS.

SNICK SNICK

Nov. 7, 2000

jon@goats.com

I'M SORRY. WHAT WAS THE QUESTION AGAIN?

IN TODAY'S SEXUALLY CHARGED WORKPLACE, MILD FLIRTATION CAN OFTEN GROW INTO SOMETHING MUCH BIGGER. SOMETHING LONG AND HARD AND THROBBING...

BEHIND the SCENES

DAY 4: SEX DWARF

I THOUGHT PHILLIP WAS JUST BEING FRIENDLY, BUT HE WANTED MORE... MUCH MORE. I WALKED OFF THE SET THE DAY HE SHOWED UP NAKED IN MY DRESSING ROOM WITH A CAN OF E-Z CHEEZ.

Nov. 8, 2000

jon@goats.com

SURE, WE TOOK IT TO COURT... BUT IT WAS SO DEGRADING. THE THINGS THEY DREDGED UP... MY WIFE WAS THERE. SHE WON'T EVEN TALK TO ME ANYMORE.

EVEN COMIC STRIP CELEBRITIES HAVE EVERYDAY PROBLEMS... EVERYDAY NEEDS. SOMETIMES HEALTH PROBLEMS GET IN THE WAY OF CARTOON SUCCESS...

BEHIND the SCENES

DAY 5: JEDI MOUSE

I JOINED GOATS BACK IN THE EARLY DAYS, BACK BEFORE IT WAS ONLY ABOUT MONEY. BUT AT LEAST WE HAD A BENEFITS PACKAGE.

Nov. 9, 2000

jon@goats.com

BUT WHEN I NEEDED MEDICAL HELP, THE INSURANCE COMPANY REJECTED MY CLAIM. THEY SAID THAT DEATH WAS A PRE-EXISTING CONDITION. I'M STILL PAYING OFF THE LOANS. $*#@!! DOCTORS.

NOT ALL THE CHARACTERS THAT HAVE LEFT OUR STRIP HAVE COME TO BAD ENDS. OCCASIONALLY, THERE'S A LIGHT AT THE END OF THE TUNNEL.

BEHIND the SCENES

DAY 6: LORI